The JOHN WAYNE Code

An American Conservative Manifesto

Compiled and Edited by
Michael Turback

HISTORY
COMPANY
BOOKS

www.johnwaynecode.com

The quotes in this book have been drawn from many sources, and are assumed to be accurate as quoted in their previously published forms. Although every effort has been made to verify the quotes and sources, the publisher cannot guarantee their perfect accuracy.

2009 Revised Edition

Printed and bound in the United States of America

THE JOHN WAYNE CODE is offered by the John Wayne Birthplace Society,
a non-profit organization which exists to preserve and expand
the birthplace of Winterset, Iowa's most famous resident.
Sales of THE JOHN WAYNE CODE at www.johnwaynebirthplace.org
support the mission of the society.

"A man's got to have a code, a creed to live by, no matter his job."

— John Wayne, American Conservative

BETRAYAL

When faced with charges of Koran desecration and other allegations by radical Muslims, State Department advisors to George W. Bush reminded the President of a quotation by John Wayne and sent him a DVD copy of the 1948 film, *She Wore a Yellow Ribbon*.

Wayne's character, Captain Nathan Brittles, facing an Indian attack, advises a junior officer: "Never apologize, son. It's a sign of weakness."

Bush, of course, never apologized or accepted blame for his actions, but throughout his failed Presidency, he might have been better served with some education in Conservative philosophy.

Today's so-called Conservatives support the idea of limited government, but they have increased government's size, power and reach to new heights. They believe in balanced budgets, but they have boosted government spending, debt, and pork to record levels. They believe in individual liberty and the rule of law, but they have condoned torture, and ignored laws passed by Congress. They have substituted religion for politics, and damaged both. They have betrayed fundamental Conservative tradition espoused by everyone from Edmund Burke to Ronald Reagan.

RUGGED INDIVIDUALIST

John Wayne was the most popular and durable star in film history, beloved as the archetype of rugged individualism, template of authentic Americanism, and, perhaps, the most authentic voice of the American Conservative movement.

Fellow actor, Katherine Hepburn, called him a political reactionary, a man who suffers from a point of view based entirely on his own experience. "He was surrounded in his early years in the motion picture business by people like himself. Self-made. Hard-working. Independent. Of the style of man who blazed the trails across our country. 'Pull your own freight.' This is their slogan."

In 1979, President Jimmy Carter mourned John Wayne's death: "He was bigger than life. In an age of few heroes, he was the genuine article. But he was more than a hero. He was a symbol of so many of the qualities that made America great. The ruggedness, the tough independence, the sense of personal courage — on and off screen — reflected the best of our national character."

"Few other men living or dead," said actor Jimmy Stewart, "have ever portrayed the fine, decent, and generous American qualities as Duke did." Maureen O'Hara insisted that he was not just an actor. "John Wayne is the United States of America," said Ms. O'Hara.

In an age of few heroes, he was the genuine article.

LESSONS LEARNED, LESSONS FORGOTTEN

On and off screen, John Wayne lived up to what he believed, based on what he knew. The simple but powerful principles he stood for are the core values we ought to embrace if we are to be successful as individuals and as a nation. Only by following his example of pride, discipline, courage, brotherhood, and respect in our personal and professional lives should we call ourselves true Conservatives.

The John Wayne Code means that you never shoot first, hit a smaller man, or take unfair advantage. You never go back on your word, and you always tell the truth. You do not advocate racially or religiously intolerant ideas, and you always help people in distress. You respect women, parents, and your nation's laws.

John Wayne would oppose pre-emptive wars and unnecessary foreign entanglements.

John Wayne would defend a citizen's right to privacy and personal liberty.

Although John Wayne believed in free enterprise, he would demand responsibility and accountability — of persons, of corporations, of institutions, and of government.

John Wayne would insist on the nation's fiscal responsibility, conscious of what we owe to future generations.

A good steward of the environment, John Wayne would do everything possible to protect the land he loved.

The ideological mess now called contemporary Conservatism stands in sharp contrast to John Wayne's essential view of American life. If you believe yourself to be a Conservative, the sentiments expressed in this collection will reveal the extent to which your modern leaders have strayed from their roots.

THE OLD MASTER

Taoism describes an ideal state as one in which a person loves his own country so much that, even though the next country is so close, and he can hear its roosters crowing and its dogs barking, he is content to die of old age without ever having gone to see it. This is the Tao of John Wayne's America.

Through his countless film roles, the wise teacher embodies individualism and perseverance in pursuit of what is right. Love of country molds him, drives and emboldens him, yet he preaches a minimum of government intervention, asking us to rely instead on individual development — the strength to transform our own lives and thereby to fulfill our mission. The Old Master never reaches for the great and thus achieves greatness.

LOADED PISTOLS

John Wayne didn't mince his words. On and off screen, he spoke in declarative, often blunt sentences to express what he meant. The effect of reading his words is to create the portrait of a man who acts out of conviction and is willing to die for his country and its virtue.

"Words are loaded pistols," wrote Jean-Paul Sartre. John Wayne's words were as powerful as the six-guns he wore on his hips.

He was type-cast throughout his movie career, playing characters whose dialog often articulated his own beliefs. Wayne himself admitted, "Regardless of character, I always play John Wayne." So blurred was the line between his personal and professional life, between art and reality— an amalgam of American culture, politics, ideals, philosophy, and attitudes — that aphorisms from his films have been accepted as part of a code of ethics. "I've killed men on the screen," he once said, "but it was always because they didn't follow the code." The John Wayne Code.

Herewith, an American icon in his own words, a refresher course on Conservative values.

Philosophy

My convictions are my own,
and I'm entitled to them.

Philosophy

A man ought to do
what he thinks is right.

Philosophy

A man's got to do
what a man's got to do.

Philosophy

Courage is being scared
to death...
and saddling up anyway.

Philosophy

When you come slam-bang
up against trouble,
it never looks half as bad
if you face up to it.

Philosophy

"Macho" is for those who feel
they have something
to prove.
Christ, how I hate that word!

Philosophy

Perversion and corruption
masquerade as ambiguity.
I don't like ambiguity.
I don't trust ambiguity.

Talk low, talk slow,
and don't say too much.

Philosophy

If you've got them by
the balls,
their hearts and minds
will follow.

Philosophy

Life is tough,
but it's tougher
when you're stupid.

Philosophy

There's always a little truth
in everything you hear.

We must always look to the future.
Tomorrow — the time that gives a
man just one more chance — is one
of the many things that I feel are
wonderful in life. So's a good horse
under you. Or the only campfire for
miles around. Or a quiet night and a
nice soft hunk of ground to sleep on.
A mother meeting her first-born.
The sound of a kid calling you dad
for the first time. There's a lot of
things great about life. But I think
tomorrow is the most important
thing. Comes in to us at midnight
very clean. It's perfect when it
arrives and it puts itself in our hands.
It hopes we've learned something
from yesterday.

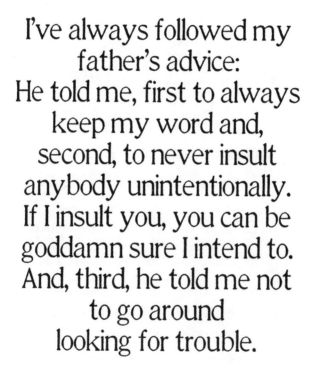

Philosophy

I've always followed my
father's advice:
He told me, first to always
keep my word and,
second, to never insult
anybody unintentionally.
If I insult you, you can be
goddamn sure I intend to.
And, third, he told me not
to go around
looking for trouble.

A horse is a horse.
It don't make a difference
what color it is.

Philosophy

Never apologize
and never explain.
It's a sign of weakness.

Philosophy

I don't like quitters,
especially when they're not
good enough to finish
what they start.

Philosophy

You've gotta believe in
what you're fighting for.

If you fight,
you fight to win.

No great trail was ever blazed
without hardship.
And you've gotta fight!
That's life.
And when you stop fighting,
that's death.

Philosophy

You give people a chance,
and then you give them
a second chance.
But after two chances,
that's it.
After you start to lose your
dignity, that's where you
have to draw the line.

There's some things a man
just can't run away from.

Philosophy

There's right
and there's wrong.
You gotta do one or the other.
You do one and you're living.
You do the other and you
may be walking around,
but in reality,
you're dead.

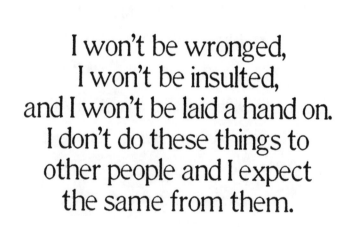

Philosophy

I won't be wronged,
I won't be insulted,
and I won't be laid a hand on.
I don't do these things to
other people and I expect
the same from them.

Philosophy

A man's only good for
one oath at a time.

Philosophy

Nobody can make me
break my word.

Philosophy

Sorry don't get it done, dude.

Philosophy

Never think anyone is
better than you,
but never assume you're
superior to anyone else.
Try to be decent to everyone,
until they give you
reason not to.

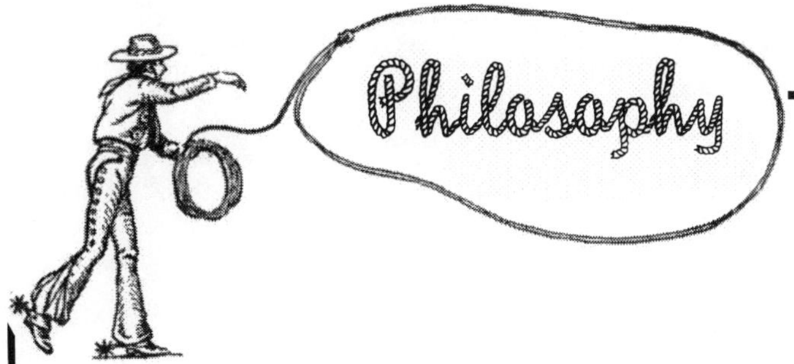

If you won't respect
your elders,
I'll teach you to respect
your betters.

Things are going to be run
my way,
and you can start adjusting
yourself to that idea.

Philosophy

You can't give the enemy
a break.
Send them to hell.

Philosophy

A man settles
his own problems.

Philosophy

You get crossways with me
and you'll think a thousand
bricks had fell on you.

Philosophy

I don't stand talking
in the wind.

Philosophy

I don't believe in surrenders.

Courage is being scared
to death
but saddling up anyway.

Philosophy

All battles are fought by
scared men who would
rather have been
somewhere else.

Philosophy

I won't be wronged,
I won't be insulted,
and I won't be laid a hand on.

Philosophy

There's no land anywhere
worth a hoot, 'til it's flowed
with good honest sweat.

Philosophy

Land and money are
the two things
that drive men mad.

Philosophy

A man ought a do
what he thinks is best.

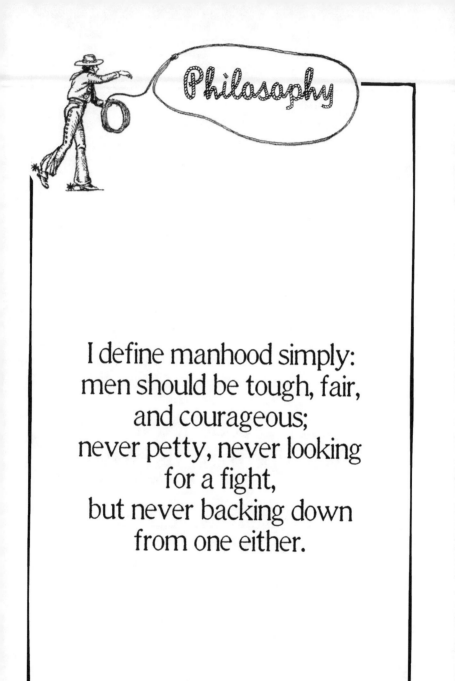

Philosophy

I define manhood simply:
men should be tough, fair,
and courageous;
never petty, never looking
for a fight,
but never backing down
from one either.

Philosophy

Everything has to end,
sometime or another.
Nothing is permanent;
only a goddamn fool
would think that
anything is forever.

Philosophy

We brought nothing
into this world,
and it's certain
we can carry nothing out.

I'm the stuff men
are made of.

On Himself

I don't have to assert
my virility.
I think my career has shown
that I'm not exactly
a pantywaist.

On Himself

I'm just an ordinary
goddamn American
and I talk for all the ordinary
goddamn Americans,
the butchers and bakers
and plumbers.
I know these people;
I know what they think.

On Himself

I have tried to live my life
so that my family
would love me
and my friends respect me.
The others can do whatever
the hell they please.

On Himself

I guess I must walk different
than other people,
but I haven't gone to
any school to learn how.

On Himself

I drink for comradeship,
and when I drink
for comradeship,
I don't bother to count.

On Himself

I'm pretty big
and got enough fat on me,
so I guess I can drink
a fair amount.

On Himself

Commemorativo tequila.
That's as fine a liquor
as there is in the world.
Christ, I tell you it's better
than any whiskey;
it's better than any schnapps;
it's better than any drink
I ever had in my life.

On Himself

I never trust a man
who doesn't drink.

On Himself

You may disagree completely
with what I say,
but I will defend to the death
my right to say it.

On Himself

It rankles me when
somebody tries
to force somebody
to do something.

On Himself

I listen to every point of view,
and then make up my mind.

On Himself

I am a demonstrative man,
a baby picker-upper,
a hugger and a kisser.
That's my nature.

On Himself

I've avoided being
mean or petty,
but I've never avoided
being rough or tough.

On Himself

A long time ago
I made me a rule.
I let people do what
they want a do.

On Himself

There've been a lot of stories
about how I got
to be called Duke.
One was that I played the
part of a duke in a school play.
Sometimes, they even said
I was descended
from royalty!
It was all a lot of rubbish.
Hell, the truth is that
I was named after a dog!

If I could choose one person
in American history
I wish I'd been,
I'd choose Sam Houston.
He had a philosophy of life
I've tried to live by.
He always wore a ring,
a ring his mother gave him.
It had a word inscribed inside:
Honor.

The one person I would most
like to spend time with is
Winston Churchill.
He's the most terrific fella
of our century.
He took a nearly beaten
nation and kept
their dignity for them.
Churchill was unparalleled.

There's been no
top authority saying
what marijuana does to you.
I really don't know that much
about it.
I tried it once but
it didn't do anything to me.

On Himself

As long as a man has
a project —something to
look forward to —they'll
always be something
important to him.
He'll never really get old.
If I had nothing to
look forward to,
I might as well be dead.

On Himself

Even grown men
need understanding.

On Himself

They say that when
a man starts growing old,
the first faculty to go,
or is it the second
(I forget which),
is the memory.

On Himself

I have tried to live my life
so that my family
would love me
and my friends respect me.
The others can do whatever
the hell they please.

On Himself

I hope that I appeal to
the more carefree times in a
person's life rather than to
his reasoning adulthood.
I'd just like to be an image
that reminds someone of joy
rather than of
the problems of the world.

On Himself

You know, I hear everybody
talking about
the generation gap.
Frankly, sometimes I don't
know what they're
talking about.
Heck, by now I should know a
little bit about it,
if I'm ever going to.
I have seven kids and
eighteen grandkids and I don't
seem to have any trouble
talking to any of them.
Never have had, and I don't
intend to start now.

On Himself

Ever since we moved to
California, I loved the sea.
More than anything else,
I wanted to go to Annapolis
and become an officer
in the Navy. It was a terrible
disappointment when I didn't
make it. In a way, I guess
I never really got over it.

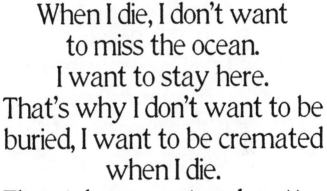

On Himself

When I die, I don't want
to miss the ocean.
I want to stay here.
That's why I don't want to be
buried, I want to be cremated
when I die.
Then take me out and scatter
me over the ocean, because
that's where my heart is.

On Himself

God, how I hate
solemn funerals.
When I die, take me into a
room and burn me.
Then my family and a few
good friends should get
together, have a few good
belts, and talk about
the crazy old time
we all had together.

On His Profession

I don't do nuance.

On His Profession

My fans expect me to be
tall in the saddle.

One look works better than
twenty lines of dialogue.
Let those actors
who picked their noses
get all the dialogue,
just give me
the close-up of reaction.

I made up my mind that
I was going to play a real man
to the best of my ability...
I was trying to play a man
who gets dirty, who sweats
sometimes, who enjoys really
kissing a gal he likes, who
gets angry, who fights clean
whenever possible but will
fight dirty if he has to.

I stick to simple themes.
Love. Hate. No nuances.
I stay away from
psychoanalyst's couch scenes.
Couches are good
for one thing.

A guy can kill, he can be mean
and vicious —and he could still
hold an audience. But let him
show a yellow streak
and he will lose them.

A hero in a movie
should never cry
in the presence of
his wife or child.

The hardest thing to do in a scene is to do nothing, or seem to do nothing, because doing nothing requires extreme work and discipline.

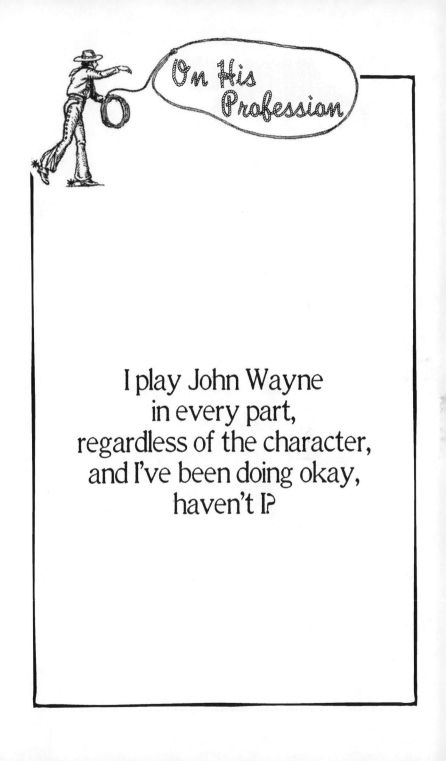

I play John Wayne
in every part,
regardless of the character,
and I've been doing okay,
haven't I?

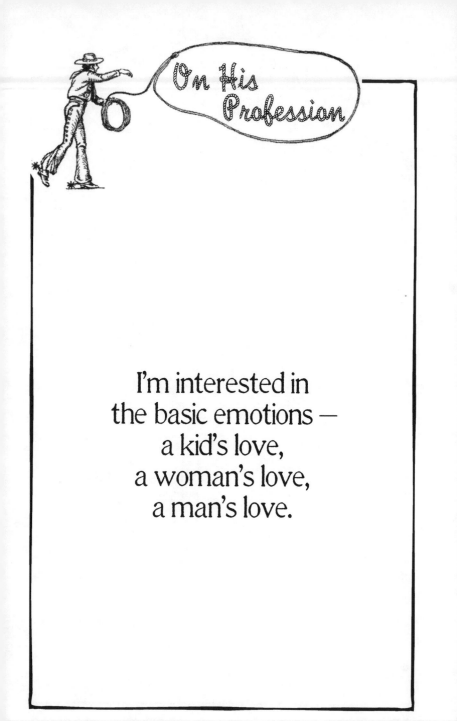

I'm interested in
the basic emotions —
a kid's love,
a woman's love,
a man's love.

There aren't going to be
any bare asses
in any movie I'm in,
particularly if
the bare ass is mine.

On His Profession

Any man who would make
an X-rated movie
ought to have to take
his daughter to see it.

I plead for guidelines
of good taste,
so that our peers may be
proud of the product carrying
the Hollywood seal,
rather than have it represent
an alphabetical gradation
of vulgarity in our pictures.

I don't ever want to appear
in a film that would
embarrass a viewer.
A man can take his wife,
mother, and daughter to one
of my movies
and never be ashamed
or embarrassed for going.

I have certain feelings
about what I do.
I like to play a character that
a large number of people can
identify with.
Whether it's that they can
say he's their father, uncle,
brother, or whatever.
It's human dignity... nothing
mean or petty, cruel or rough.
Tough, that's all right.

I've worked in a business
where it's almost
a requirement
to break your word
if you want to survive,
but whenever I signed a
contract for five years or for
a certain amount of money,
I've always lived up to it.

The best action a man can do
is get on a horse
and chase a bad guy.
More action for a man than
anything he could do.
It's better than gettin' in a
tank and stickin' your head
out and shootin' a gun.
It's good, raw action.

All I do is sell sincerity, and
I've been selling the hell out
of that since I started...
I was never one of
the little theatre boys.
That arty crowd has only
surface brilliance anyway.
Real art is basic emotion.
If a scene is handled with
simplicity —and I don't mean
simple —it'll be good and
the public will know it.

On His Profession

The older I get,
the more popular I become.

On His Profession

I stopped getting the girl
about ten years ago —
which is just as well
because I'd forgotten
what I wanted her for.

On His Profession

I merely try to act naturally.
If I start acting phony on the
screen, you start looking at
me instead of feeling with me.
But you can't be natural;
you have to act natural,
because if you're just natural
you can drop a scene.

In a bad picture, you see them
acting all over the place.
In a good picture, they react in
a logical way to a situation
they're in, so the audience can
identify with the actors.

On His Profession

I read dramatic lines
undramatically
and react to situations
normally.

You can't eat awards.
Nor, more to the point
drink them.
I really didn't need an Oscar.
I'm a box-office champion
with a record they're going
to have to run to catch.
And they won't.

I'm an American actor.
I work with my clothes on.
I have to.
Riding a horse can be
pretty tough on your legs
and elsewheres.

On His Profession

The violence in my pictures
is lusty
and a little bit humorous,
because I believe
humor nullifies violence.

High Noon is the most
un-American movie
I've ever seen.
I resented that scene when
the marshal ripped off
his badge and threw it on
the ground. That was like
belittling a medal of honor.

On His Profession

People should not go
to the movies
unless they believe in heroes.

On His Profession

The critics have drawn up
a caricature of me,
which doesn't bother me.
Their opinions don't matter
to the people who go to
the movies.

On His Profession

Nobody liked my acting
but the public.

On His Profession

If I depended on the critics'
judgment and recognition,
I'd never have gone into the
motion picture business.

I've played the kind of man
I'd like to have been.

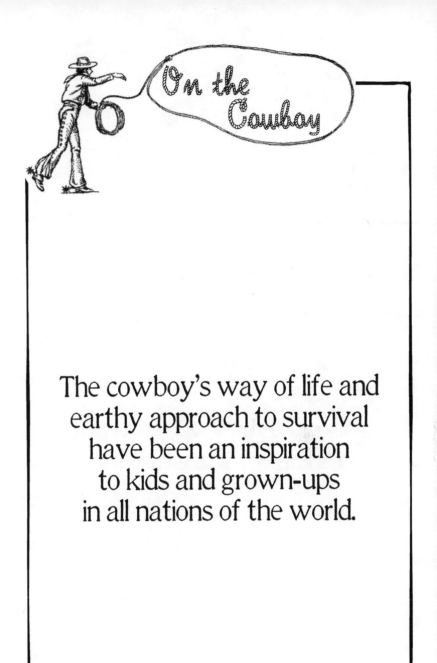

On the Cowboy

The cowboy's way of life and
earthy approach to survival
have been an inspiration
to kids and grown-ups
in all nations of the world.

On the Cowboy

Nobody ever saw a cowboy
on the psychiatrist's couch.

Every country in the world
loved the folklore of the West
—the music, the dress, the
excitement, everything that
was associated with the
opening of a new territory.
It took everybody out of their
own little world. The cowboy
lasted a hundred years,
created more songs and prose
and poetry than any other
folk figure. The closest thing
was the Japanese samurai.
I wonder who'll continue it.

On the Cowboy

The West.
The very words go straight to
that place of the heart where
Americans feel the spirit of
pride in their western heritage
—the triumph of personal
courage over any obstacle,
whether nature or man.

On the Cowboy

Westerns are closer to art
than anything else in
the motion picture business.

On the
Cowboy

Put a man on a horse,
and right off you've got
the making of
something magnificent.
Physical strength, speed
where you can feel it,
plus heroism. And the hero,
he's big and strong.

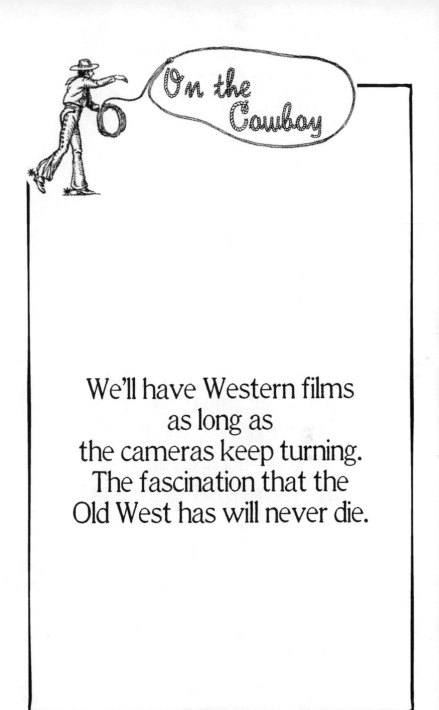

On the Cowboy

We'll have Western films
as long as
the cameras keep turning.
The fascination that the
Old West has will never die.

On the Sexes

I like women,
and I've probably been
a lot softer than I should be
on occasion with them.
And a lot tougher on
some men, mainly myself.

On the Sexes

Getting rid of a man without
hurting his masculinity
is a problem.
"Get out" and "I never want
to see you again" might
sound like a challenge.
If you want to get rid of a
man, I suggest saying, "I love
you.... I want to marry you....
I want to have your children."
Sometimes they leave
skid marks.

Men need instant replays
in sports.
They've already forgotten
what happened.

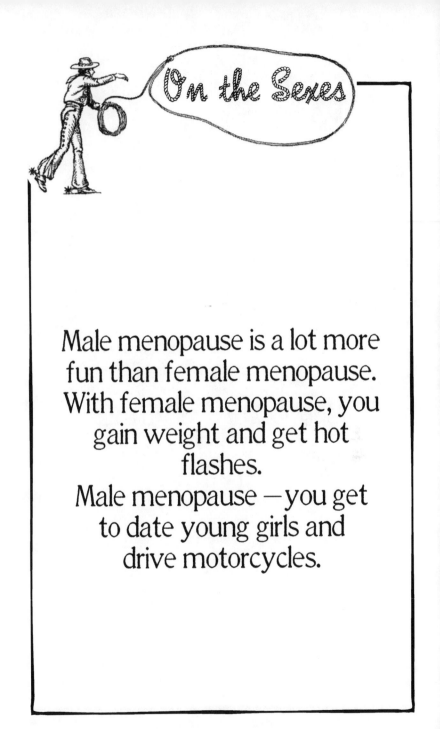

On the Sexes

Male menopause is a lot more fun than female menopause. With female menopause, you gain weight and get hot flashes.
Male menopause —you get to date young girls and drive motorcycles.

On the Sexes

Men *forget* everything;
women *remember*
everything.

On the Sexes

I think women's lib is fine,
as long as they're home
by six to cook my dinner.

On the Sexes

Most men hate to shop.
That's why the
men's department is
usually on the first floor
of a department store,
two inches from the door.

On the Sexes

Men like to barbecue.
Men will cook
if danger is involved.

All men hate to hear
"We need to talk
about our relationship."
These seven words strike
fear in the heart of even
General Schwartzkopf.

On the Sexes

If a man says, "I'll call you,"
and he doesn't,
he didn't forget.
He didn't lose your number.
He didn't die.
He just didn't want
to call you.

On the Sexes

I've had three wives,
six children,
and six grandchildren,
and I still don't
understand women.

On the Sexes

I don't know much
about thoroughbreds,
horses, or women.

On the Sexes

I've never met a woman yet
that was half as reliable
as a horse.

On the Sexes

I'm a guy who likes girls,
all kinds of girls.

On the Sexes

Any woman who devotes
herself to making
one man miserable,
instead of a lot of men happy,
don't get my vote.

On the Sexes

No nation on earth has a
monopoly on beauty.
But I consider the women of
South and Central America
to be unusually
warm and lovely.
They have a good feeling
for family life.
They respect their husbands,
and they respect
their marriages.

On the Sexes

I guess I've been
a romantic all my life.
A romantic about everything,
not just about women.
I will have to learn to drop
that pedestal a few feet so
I can accept women on a
more realistic basis.

On the Sexes

As far as a man and a woman
are concerned,
I'm awfully happy
there's a thing called sex.
It's an extra something
God gave us...
Healthy, lusty sex
is wonderful.

On the Sexes

I taught you what to do
when the snow comes,
how to survive in a blizzard.
And, I taught you how to deal
with men, but women,
nobody knows what's on a
woman's mind.

I can tell you why I love her (his wife Pilar). I have a lust for her dignity. I look at her wonderfully classic face, and I see hidden in it a sense of humor that I love. I think of wonderful, exciting, decent things when I look at her.

On the Sexes

I've never in my life worked with a woman who had the smell of drama that Katherine Hepburn has. She's so feminine. She's a man's woman.

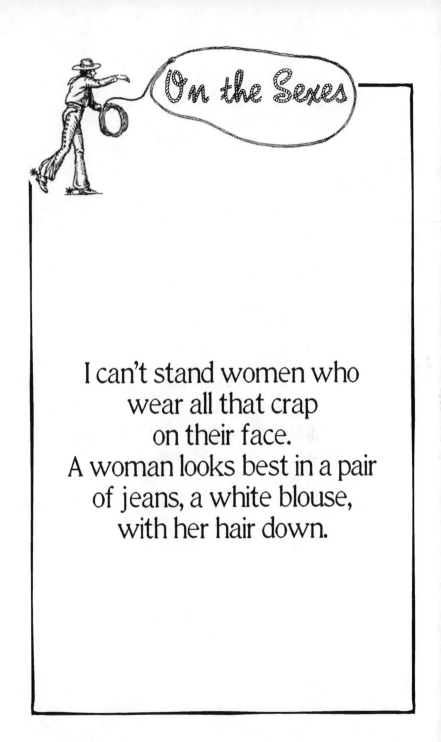

On the Sexes

I can't stand women who
wear all that crap
on their face.
A woman looks best in a pair
of jeans, a white blouse,
with her hair down.

On the Sexes

No woman is going to get me hog-tied and branded.

On the Sexes

Women. Peculiar.

On Faith

Believing in God is different
than drooling over
rubies and emeralds.

I've always had deep faith
that there is a Supreme Being,
there has to be. To me that's
just a normal thing to have
that kind of faith. The fact
that He's let me stick around
a little longer, or She's let me
stick around a little longer,
certainly goes great with me,
and I want to hang around as
long as I'm healthy and
not in anybody's way.

On Faith

I don't belong to any church.
I believe in
God and Jesus Christ,
and I pray.
If anything, I guess I'm a
Presby-goddamn-terian.

On Faith

When the road looks rough
ahead, remember
the Man Upstairs
and the word H-O-P-E.
Hang onto both
and tough it out.

On Faith

I know the man upstairs will pull the plug when he wants to, but I don't want to end up my life being sick. I want to go out on two feet —in action.

On Faith

The best four-letter word is
H-O-P-E.

On Faith

Jesus Christ was Jewish, at least he started out Jewish.

On Faith

Sure I licked the big C.
But I did not do it by myself.
I had good surgeons
and a good team
and a good hospital.
Yes, and I prayed to God.

On Faith

There must be some
higher power or how else
does all this work?

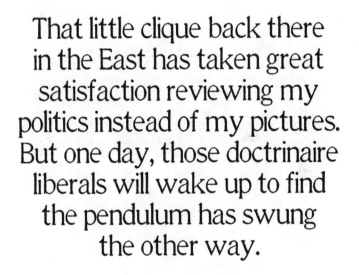

That little clique back there
in the East has taken great
satisfaction reviewing my
politics instead of my pictures.
But one day, those doctrinaire
liberals will wake up to find
the pendulum has swung
the other way.

On Politics

I'm aware that I'm unpopular
in the industry because my
political philosophy is different
from the prevailing attitude.
But I don't reply when they
gang up on me, because
I think political street fighting
is unprofessional.

On Politics

The Constitution was meant
for honest, descent citizens.
I resent the fact that it can be
used and abused by
the very people
who want to destroy it.

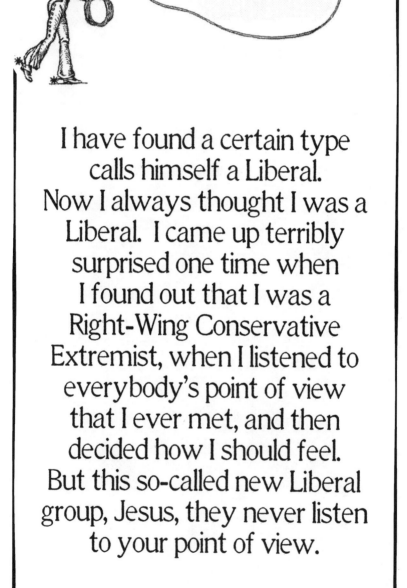

On Politics

I have found a certain type
calls himself a Liberal.
Now I always thought I was a
Liberal. I came up terribly
surprised one time when
I found out that I was a
Right-Wing Conservative
Extremist, when I listened to
everybody's point of view
that I ever met, and then
decided how I should feel.
But this so-called new Liberal
group, Jesus, they never listen
to your point of view.

On Politics

Nobody's enjoying this war (Vietnam), but it happens to be damned necessary. Ever since the Soviet Revolution of 1917, the Communists haven't compromised once in the family of nations. They're out to destroy us, and logic should tell us that this Vietnam war is the only right course. Besides — we gave our word.

On Politics

The anti-war movement is an articulate minority who attract more attention than their numbers warrant.

When I saw what our boys
are going through — and how
the morale was holding up,
and the job they were doing,
I just knew they had
to make this picture
(*The Green Berets*).

On Politics

If we're going to send
one man to die,
we ought to make it
an all-out conflict.

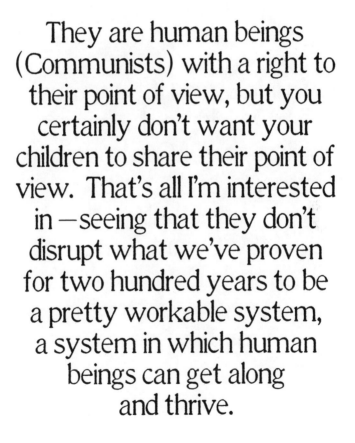

They are human beings
(Communists) with a right to
their point of view, but you
certainly don't want your
children to share their point of
view. That's all I'm interested
in — seeing that they don't
disrupt what we've proven
for two hundred years to be
a pretty workable system,
a system in which human
beings can get along
and thrive.

On Politics

I wouldn't mind if they taught my children the basic philosophy of Communism, in theory and how it works in actuality.
But I don't want somebody like Angela Davis inculcating an enemy doctrine in my kids' minds.

On Politics

This new thing of
genuflecting to
the downtrodden, I don't go
along with that. We ought to
go back to praising the kids
who get good grades, instead
of making excuses for
the ones who shoot the
neighborhood groceryman.

On Politics

I'm against these people
who carry placards to save
the life of some criminal,
yet have no thought for
the innocent victim.

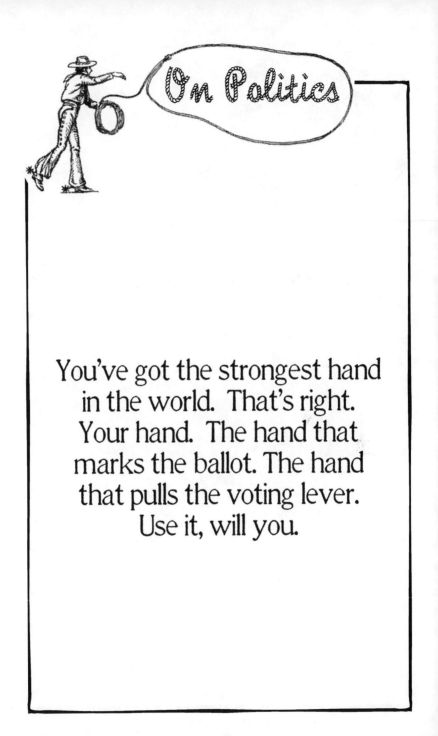

On Politics

You've got the strongest hand in the world. That's right. Your hand. The hand that marks the ballot. The hand that pulls the voting lever. Use it, will you.

On Politics

To hell with the press.

On Politics

This guy (Ted Kennedy) says he only cares about the issues. Bullshit. He cares about getting power, and he'll say and do whatever he has to to get it — just like every other politician. If he'd just admit he's like everyone else. Ted Kennedy's so fake he makes me sick.

I think that loud roar of
irresponsible liberalism, which
in the old days we called
radicalism, is being quieted
down by a reasoning public.
I think the pendulum's
swinging back.
We're remembering that
the past can't be so bad.
We built a nation on it.

On Country

This nation is more than
laws and government.
It's an outlook, an attitude.

On Country

"Republic." I like the sound of the word. It means people can live free, talk free. Go or come, buy or sell, be drunk or sober, however they choose.

Some words give ya a feeling. "Republic" is one of those words that makes me tight in the throat. The same tightness a man gets when his baby takes his first step, or his first baby shaves, makes his first sound like a man. Some words can give you a feeling that makes your heart warm. "Republic" is one of those words.

On Country

I'm quite sure that the concept of a government-run (Indian) reservation would have an ill effect on anyone. But that's what the socialists are looking for now — to have everyone cared for from cradle to grave.

On Country

Give the American people
a good cause, and there's
nothing they can't lick.

On Country

We've made mistakes along
the way, but that's no reason
to start tearing up
the best flag God ever gave
to any country.

On Country

No one stays as he was —
nor any country.

On Country

I think government is
a necessary evil,
like, say,
motion-picture agents.

On Country

I don't feel we did wrong in
taking this great country
away from them.
There were great numbers of
people who needed new land,
and the Indians were
selfishly trying to keep it
for themselves.

Sure I wave
the American flag.
Do you know a better flag
to wave? Sure I love my
country with all her faults.
I'm not ashamed of that,
never have been,
never will be.

On Country

We've made mistakes along
the way, but that's no reason
to start tearing up the best
flag God ever gave
to any country.

On Country

I never felt I needed to
apologize for my patriotism.
I felt that if there were
Communists in the business
(show business) —and I knew
there were —then they ought
to go over to Russia and try
enjoying freedom there.

On Country

My hope and prayer is that everyone know and love our country for what she really is and what she stands for.

On Country

I hope that seeing the battle
of the Alamo will remind
Americans that liberty and
freedom don't come cheap.
I hope our children will get a
sense of our glorious past, and
appreciate the struggle our
ancestors made for the
precious freedoms we now
enjoy —and sometimes just
kind of take for granted.

On Country

I wish they would re-release
The Alamo today.
There's more to that movie
than my damn
conservative attitude.

As a country, our yesterdays
tell us that we have to win
not only at war but at peace.

On Country

"My Country 'Tis of Thee"
gives me goosepimples.